MIYUKI

The History of Delica Beads

The popularity of Delica Beads® by MIYUKI for stunning jewelry and bead bags has become widespread. It began with the founding of a Japanese bead company in the 1930s. With a small variety of initial bead types, MIYUKI first produced only transparent and opaque small beads.

While MIYUKI worked toward improvements in quality, beaded bags and beaded dresses grew in demand. Around 1960, Japan's Empress Michiko used a bead embroidery bag that triggered a wave of popularity. Beads of higher quality with an increase in the number of colors were produced. MIYUKI also developed plating technology for silver lined beads.

Regarding the birth of Delica beads, customers inquired about the feasibility of producing beads which were suitable for weaving in terms of shape. Beaders wanted small, delicate and elegant beads for bead bags like the ones cherished by noblewomen in Europe in the 19th century.

With an eye toward this, MIYUKI developed beads suitable in shape... cylindrical beads which are uniform in shape with large holes (allowing several strings to pass through).

The most difficult part in manufacturing these beads was cutting. Since the thickness of the glass is thin, glass is easily broken and it becomes very hard to cut glass tubes. As a result of continuous trial and error, it became feasible to make innovative beads which are uniform in shape by developing a special cutting machine and devising a method of heating to cut pieces evenly. MIYUKI named these elegant and exquisite beads "Delica Beads." The name was adopted from the word delicacy in English.

Delica bead weaving evoked enthusiasm in Japan and in the U.S. MIYUKI began to teach "Delica bead weaving" and establish schools to popularize it. They educated beaders, trained teachers, and established the "Delica Bead Loom Association" in Japan. The Association is in its 23rd year with members totaling 4,500 people and 500 teachers.

Looking back, the progress of the development of Delica beads and the opening of the MIYUKI bead factory have led to increased bead enthusiasts.

Index

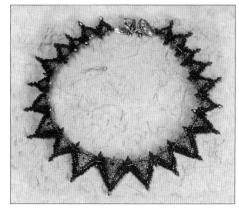
CW00543036

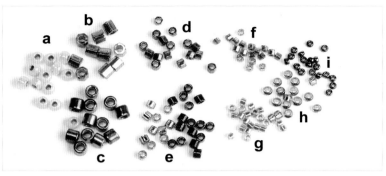

Delica Bead Shapes and Sizes

Beads from left to right: (a) Miyuki size 8/0 seed bead, #198, copper-lined satin; (b) Delica size 8/0 cut, DBL89C, luster black-lined amber; (c) Delica size 8/0 plain, DBL29, metallic purple/gold iris; (d) Delica size 10/0 cut, DBM103C, dusty rose with gold luster; (e) Delica size 10/0, DBM146, silver-lined light amethyst transparent; DBM105, light luster transparent crimson; (f) Delica size 11/0 cut, DB89C, luster black-lined amber; (g) Delica size 11/0, DB58, luster blue-lined clear; (h) Miyuki size 11/0 seed bead, #12, silver-lined light amethyst transparent; (i) Miyuki size 15/0 seed bead, #455, black iris AB.

	Bead	size	type	width in mm	length in mm
●	Delica	8/0	cut	3.0	3.0
●	Delica	8/0	plain	3.0	3.0
●	Round	8/0		3.0	2.0
●	Delica	10/0	cut	2.2	1.7
●	Delica	10/0	plain	2.2	1.7
●	Round	11/0		2.0	1.4
●	Delica	11/0	cut	1.6	1.4
●	Delica	11/0	plain	1.6	1.4
●	Round	15/0		1.5	1.0

Delica beads, also known generically as Japanese cylinder beads, are cylindrical in shape and very regular. They were invented by Mr. Masayoshi Katsuoka, president of Miyuki Company, in the early 1980s, and the original size, 11/0, arrived in the United States in 1987. Size 8/0 followed in the mid-1990s. And Miyuki developed the new size 10/0 within the last year.

All three sizes come in both the original plain cylinder and the hexagonal or "cut" shape. You will find very few irregular beads in packages of size 10 and 11 plain Delicas. Size 8/0 Delicas evince slightly more irregularity; and while cuts have been fire polished to produce smooth edges, a few may have sharp ends, so choose them with care.

In fact, to get the best results, you should always select Delicas and other kinds of beads carefully; even in the most regular of brands there will always be slight size and length variations in a package.

Seed beads are measured across the width of their hole (the diameter) to determine size. The length of the hole is irrelevant to their size; although it has a major impact on what kinds of beads can be used together. Using different length beads together, however, can create remarkable texture.

The type of finish applied to the bead may also affect its size slightly. Even glass type has an effect on size – black beads of any type are almost always a bit smaller than other colors of the same type for example.

In the photo, beads a, b, and c at left are all size 8/0. Notice the two a and b beads that are aligned hole to hole in the photo. While their width is almost identical, the difference in their length is dramatic. Size 8/0 round seed beads (a) average about 2.9mm in width but are about 2mm in length. Cut (b) and plain (c) size 8/0 Delicas average 2.9 to 3.05mm in width but are almost 1mm longer than round size 8/0s.

Beads d & e are size 10/0 Delicas; the d beads are cuts & the e beads are plain. Cut size 10/0 Delicas average 2.05mm in width & 1.65mm in length. Plain size 10/0 Delicas are a hair narrower & longer. Size 10/0 Delicas are closest in size to size 11/0 round Japanese seed beads (h), which average 2.15mm in width but are about 0.3mm shorter. The similarity in size of 10/0 Delicas & 11/0 Miyuki seeds makes them suitable to be used together.

Size 11/0 Delicas (f cuts & g) are markedly smaller than size 11/0 seed beads (h) but only a little larger than size 15/0 seed beads (i), revealed by the adjacent f & i beads lying on their sides. Delica size 11/0 beads (f & g) average 1.7mm in width & 1.4mm in length. Size 15/0 round seed beads (i) vary a lot in any given package but average 1.6mm in width & 1mm in length.

Threads

You should, of course, use your favorite needles and threads. Many beaders swear by the strength of Fireline, but I haven't used it since a piece I'd woven on Fireline came apart in a million pieces. I was a Nymo beader until very recently Kobayashi introduced the same new nylon filament thread in slightly different palettes. Kobayashi's new thread is K-O. The weight is similar to Nymo B, but the thread has a slick coating that causes it to resist fraying without needing any type of thread conditioner (beeswax or Thread Heaven). It also seems to be comparable in strength to Nymo D. K-O has recently produced a D weight that seems much stronger than Nymo D.

K-O and Nymo both need to be prestretched before you begin to weave. K-O is very stretchy, so prestretching will prevent your beadwork from becoming loose over time. It also uncoils the thread, which helps minimize tangling. As with any thread, you should thread the needle with the end that comes off the spool first so you are sewing with the thread's grain to minimize fraying.

If you are using beads with sharp edges, such as crystals or some cuts, you may prefer to use Fireline or Power Pro (BeadCats sells a generic version of the latter at a much reduced price). I used K-O for all the projects in this book.

Needles

The large holes in all Delica sizes make it possible to work many of these projects with size 10 beading needles.

However, you will have to use size 12 or 13 needles for projects that incorporate seed beads or have many thread passes, like "Jewel of the Pyramids."

Scissors and Glue

My favorite beading scissors are high-quality, Solingen steel manicure scissors. They're very sharp, sturdy, and come to a tiny point. Good-quality "stork" embroidery scissors also work well. When cutting off thread tails, use a trick Virginia Blakelock teaches and pull on the thread as you cut it. This stretches it slightly so the end hides inside the last bead. Never cut a thread immediately after a knot; pass it through a few beads before cutting, or the knot will come untied.

If you use clear nail polish as glue for your knots, apply a drop from the tip of your beading needle directly on the knot (another Virginia Blakelock trick). Never use the nail polish brush; the solvent could damage bead color or finish. I recommend G-S Hypo Cement for knots at the end of pearl strands.

Basic Knots

Surgeon's Knot

The surgeon's knot starts like a square knot.
1. Cross the left-hand end on top of the right-hand end, wrap it behind the right-hand cord, and bring it back to the front (lower blue line). The right-hand tail (red) now points left and the left-hand tail points right.
2. Bend the right-hand tail (red) back toward the right and the left-hand tail back toward the left (middle of knot).
3. Cross the tail that's currently on the right (blue), over the tail coming from the left (red).
4. Wrap it behind that tail and pull it through the opening between the step 1 cross and the step 3 cross (this is a square knot).
5. To turn it into a surgeon's knot wrap behind, under, and through to the front again. The result is that the top of the knot curves partway down the sides of the first cross, which makes it more stable and unlikely to twist out of the square when you tighten it.
6. Pull the tails in the directions they are pointing to tighten knot.

 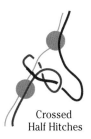 

Pair of Half Hitches   Crossed Half Hitches   Double Half Hitches

Half-Hitch Knot

1. For a plain half hitch, bring the needle through a bead. Then sew under the thread between this bead and the next bead. Tighten until a small loop remains.
2. Pass the needle through the loop, going over the thread that you previously sewed under (lower loop in pair of half hitches).
3. Repeat the process for a paired half hitch, which is more secure than a single half hitch.
4. For a crossed half hitch, repeat step 1 of the plain half hitch. Give the starting loop a half twist so its sides cross (red loop on right), then sew through it. Tighten carefully so it doesn't lock too soon.
5. Start a double half hitch like a plain half hitch but sew through the loop twice. This knot is prone to tightening prematurely.

Front-Back-Front Knot

1. Bring both cord ends through a bead and tie the first half of a square knot in front of the doubled cord that passes through the beads: right over left and through the loop on the left side.
2. Flip the strand of beads over and tie the other half of the square knot on the other side of the cords (left over right).
3. Flip the strand over again and tie half a square knot in front of the cords as in step 1.
4. Pass both ends through the next bead. Repeat.

Basic Techniques
Brick Stitch

Ladder (figure 1)

1. Pick up 2 beads and sew through them again in the same order. Nudge them into a side-by-side position. The thread exits the bottom of bead #2.
2. Pick up bead #3. Sew down bead #2 (toward the thread) then back through bead #3 in the same direction as before (up). The thread exits its top.
3. Pick up bead #4 and sew up bead #3 (toward the thread). Then sew down bead #4.
Repeat step 2 for odd-number beads and step 3 for even-number beads.
    Note: To firm up and reinforce your ladder, you can zigzag up and down beads back to bead #1 if you wish; do not do this for any of the projects in this book.

Joining a Ladder into a Tube (figure 2)

1. With the thread exiting the last ladder bead, bring the end and beginning beads of the ladder together. Make sure the ladder is not twisted.
2. If the thread is exiting the bottom of the last ladder bead, as shown here, sew bottom to top through the first ladder bead. (If the thread exits the top of the last bead, sew down the first.)
3. Sew back through the last ladder bead from top to bottom as shown.
4. Sew back up the first bead.

Brick Stitch (figures 3 and 4)

    This method prevents thread from showing on the edge of the triangle. Each row is one bead shorter than the row below.

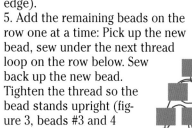

1. After completing a flat ladder with the thread exiting the top of the last bead, pick up 2 beads for the first brick stitch row.
2. Skip the nearest thread loop on the ladder (between the edge 2 beads) and sew under the loop between beads #2 and #3.
3. Sew back through the new beads, second bead first. Tighten the thread.
4. Sew through new bead #2 toward #1 so your needle is exiting the last bead added. As you tighten the thread, jiggle it to make the 2 beads assume a vertical position (figure 3, right-hand edge).
5. Add the remaining beads on the row one at a time: Pick up the new bead, sew under the next thread loop on the row below. Sew back up the new bead. Tighten the thread so the bead stands upright (figure 3, beads #3 and 4 at top left).

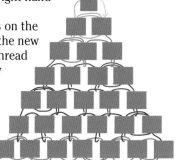

Ndebele Herringbone

Herringbone stitch works up quickly because you add two beads at a time. In other words, each stitch consists of two beads.

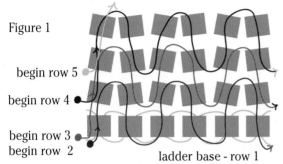

Figure 1

begin row 5
begin row 4
begin row 3
begin row 2

ladder base - row 1

Tubular Herringbone with a Ladder Base (figure 1)

The trick to successful tubular herringbone is the step up between rows. If you forget it, your tube will become skewed.

1. Start by making a ladder with an even number of beads (do not reinforce it). Then join the ladder into a ring (see "Brick stitch," p. 5, fig. 2 in Basic Techniques).
2. For the first herringbone row but the second row of the piece, come out a ladder bead, pick up 2 beads. Sew down the second ladder bead (figure 1, red dot at left and line).
3. Sew up the third ladder bead, pick up 2 beads, and sew down the fourth ladder bead.
4. Repeat around until you have sewn down the last ladder bead (orange arrow at right).
5. To begin the next row (#3), you need to sew up through the first herringbone bead added. However, since your needle is pointing down through the last bead on the row below (orange arrow at right), you need to "step up" to reach the first row 2 bead. So sew up the first ladder bead and the first herringbone bead (orange dot at left).
6. With your needle exiting the first herringbone bead, pick up 2 beads and sew down the second herringbone bead. Sew up the third and repeat around (orange line). You will end with your needle pointing down through the last row 2 bead (burgundy arrow).
7. Sew up the bead next to the one your needle is exiting (the first row 2 bead) and continue up the first bead of row 3 (burgundy dot and line).
8. For row 4, add pairs of beads over the pairs of row 3. At the end of the row you are going down the last row 3 bead (wheat arrow), so step up through the first row 3 and 4 beads to begin row 5 (wheat dot and line).
Note: If you look closely at the thread path in figure 1, you'll notice that the bead pairs of the top two rows separate from each other. Each new row pulls the pairs on the row below together. Normally, you join the pairs on the final row by working a ladder thread path through the beads (see "Beaded Gems Necklace" - page 11).

Tubular Herringbone with a Herringbone Base

1. Sew a stop bead to the thread about 6" (15cm) from the end. Then string 4 times as many beads as the number of stitches in your tube. (If you are working with a color pattern, notice how the beads stack in figure 3.) In this case, the tube will have 4 stitches, so string 16 beads (figure 2, orange line).
2. Sew back through #15 toward the start and pick up 2 beads for the third row of the first stitch. Be careful not to split any threads.
3. Sew through #14. Skip #13 and #12 and sew through #11. Pick up 2 beads and sew through #10.
4. Skip #9 and #8 and sew through #7. Pick up 2 beads and sew through #6.
5. Skip #5 and #4 and sew through #3. Pick up the 2 beads for the fourth stitch and sew through #2 and #1 (figure 2, red line).

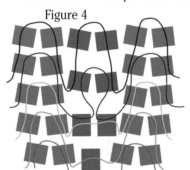

Figure 3

2 3 6 7 10 11 14 15
1 4 5 8 9 12 13 16

6. Pull both threads to gather the beads into 4 stitches 3 rows high and pinch the beads between your thumb and index finger to prevent the strip from becoming twisted (figure 3).
7. To join the strip into a tube, sew up beads #16, #15, and the first new bead (wheat-colored line in figure 3).
8. Now work in regular tubular herringbone as shown in figure 1. Don't forget to step up to begin each new round.

Increasing Herringbone

An increase is completed in three rows of Ndebele Herringbone.

Figure 4

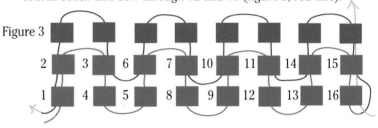

1. On the first increase round, add the 2 beads for the stitch before the increase and sew down the bead below the second bead of the new stitch. Pick up 1 bead. Sew up the first bead of the next stitch and add the two beads (figure 4, light orange line).
2. When you get to the increase point on the second row, add the 2 beads before the increase and go down the bead below. Pick up 2 beads and come up the first bead of the next stitch. Work the stitch (wheat line).
3. On the third row, transform the 2 increase beads with horizontal holes into a herringbone stitch. After making the stitch before the increase and sewing down the bead below, sew through the first increase bead. Pick up 2 beads and sew through the second increase bead. Then sew up the bead for the next regular stitch (red line).

The increase beads will tip up like a regular herringbone stitch. Note: the increase will be slightly below the level of the other stitches but will even out to the same level in another row or two (burgundy line).

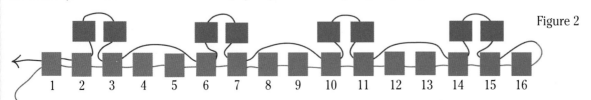

Figure 2

1 2 3 4 5 6 7 8 9 10 11 12 13 14 15 16

Peyote Stitch or Gourd Stitch

Tubular Peyote Stitch - Even Count

1. String an even number of beads that will fit around the object to be covered (figure 1, dark green beads). Tie the beads together into a ring, leaving a tiny bit of slack, and go through the first bead again (lower goldenrod line).

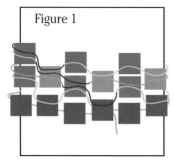

Figure 1

Note: the odd numbered beads make up row 2 and the even-numbered beads row 1.

2. For row 3, pick up a bead (medium green), skip the second strung bead, and go through the third. Pick up a bead, skip the next strung bead, and go through the next. Continue around. The last bead you pick up for the row will fit over the last strung bead (lower yellow line).

3. There is no clear "up" (raised) bead to sew through at the end of the row. Instead, you must "step up" by going through the first bead of the previous row and the first new bead of this row (bottom red line). You are now in position to add the first bead of row 4.

4. For row 4 (light green beads and second gold-enrod line), pick up a bead and go through the second bead added on row 3. Continue around, adding beads over the row 2 beads and sewing through row 3 beads.

5. The last row 4 bead will go over the first strung bead and there won't be a clear attachment point after it. Step up by sewing through the first row 3 bead and the first row 4 bead (middle red line).

6. Pick up the first row 5 bead (blue and top yellow line) and go through the second row 4 bead. Repeat around in this manner. Then step up at the end of the row by sewing through the first bead added on the previous row, 4, and the first bead added on the row you are completing, 5 (top red line).

   Notice that the step up moves one bead in the direction that you are sewing on each round.

Flat Peyote Stitch - Odd Count

1. Start with a stop bead. Then string an odd number of beads for rows 1 and 2. The odd-numbered beads form row 1 and the even-numbered beads make up row 2 and are shown half a bead higher in figure 2.

2. Pick up the first bead for row 3 (blue-green). Position it above the last bead strung and sew through the next-to-last bead.

3. Pick up a bead, skip a bead, and sew through the next bead. The last bead you pick up will sit over the first bead and there will be no following bead to which you can anchor it.

4. To fix its position you must work what is called "the hard turn," which really isn't as difficult as the name implies.

a. Sew through the first three beads strung in the original order – away from the stop bead (red line).

b. Sew through the bead above #3 toward the stop bead (red line).

c. Then continue through beads #2 and #1 (burgundy line).

d. Finally, sew through the last bead added on row 3 away from the stop bead (burgundy line). Your needle is exiting an "up" bead.

5. Work row 4 (light green) by picking up a bead and going through the next row 3 bead. Repeat across the row.

6. At the end of row 4 you will have anchored the last bead by sewing through the edge bead on row 3, so the turn to begin row 5 is easy. Just pick up a bead and sew through the last row 4 bead toward the stop bead.

7. Continue picking up row 5 beads and going through row 4 beads. The row will end like row 3 with no place to anchor the last bead (figure 2, arrow at top left).

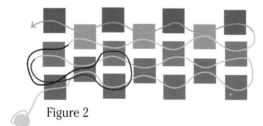

Figure 2

8. You can work a simpler "hard turn" at the end of all the odd-numbered rows after the first:

a. Sew through the edge bead and the bead diagonally below it away from the stop bead (figure 3, orange dot and line).

b. Turn and sew through the bead above the second bead and the edge bead you went through in step a (orange line to red line).

c. Now sew through the new bead at the end of the last row, working away from the stop bead (red line).

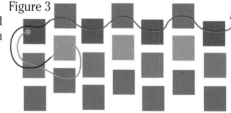

Figure 3

9. Work the easy turn at the end of even-numbered rows and the modified hard turn at the end of odd-numbered rows (the edge with the stop bead).

Crimping

You can press a crimp flat with chain-nose pliers, but crimping pliers fold the crimp so it is less visible and slightly more secure. The jaws of crimping pliers have two stations. The one closer to the handles looks like a crescent moon, and the one at the end of the pliers is oval.

1. Separate the wires in the crimp with one hand and place the crimp in the crescent moon station of the pliers (photo 1). Press firmly. The goal is to have one wire on each side of the dent that this station puts into the crimp.

2. Turn the dented crimp sideways so the dent is centered between the pliers jaws in the oval station (photo 2).

3. Press down smoothly to fold the crimp at the dent (photo 3). For security, you may want to press the fold together with chain-nose pliers.

Beaded Gems

Use tubular herringbone, graduated bead sizes, and pearls to create elegant baubles.

I love making beaded beads, and it seems as though every book I write has to include a new one. If there is one fault to my beaded beads, it's that most of them are time-consuming. So this time, I decided to create beads that look complex but can be completed in less than an hour – even the largest. Making these beads is pure fun.

I chose three colors of Delica beads, some hex-cut and some plain, and all three sizes of each color. That way, I could vary them in a vast number of ways but always end up with a pleasing result and a bowl of beads that all look good together.

The most important thing to remember when stringing beaded beads into jewelry is to place a neutral space between each bead. Plain spacer beads let the viewer's eye rest between the wealth of color and texture so she can pause to enjoy each of the beaded beads, rather than being overwhelmed and confused by their complexity.

In addition, if you're taking the time to make 21 or more beaded beads, don't skimp on finishing. A stunning clasp complements all your hard work and declares that your necklace is a work of art from start to finish. I used a sterling silver clasp set with a faceted mystic topaz from Pacific Silverworks. The clasp is simple but elegant and the mystic topaz has just the right color and sparkle to complement the Delicas.

If you don't want to make 21 (or more) beaded beads, you can create a beautiful necklace that includes only a few beaded beads as focal points. Another option is to make the smallest bicone and round beaded beads for a bracelet, but remember that bracelets take a lot of abuse, so don't wear a beaded bead bracelet for everyday.

Materials

8-10g Size 8 Delicas, hex-cut, black with rainbow luster #5C (dark/D)
8-10g Size 10 Delicas, black with rainbow luster #5 (dark/D)
8-10g Size 11 Delicas, black with rainbow luster #5 (dark/D)
8-10g Size 8 Delicas, hex-cut, amber, black-lined with rainbow luster #89C (medium/M)
8-10g Size 10 Delicas, amber, black-lined with rainbow luster #89 (medium/M)
8-10g Size 11 Delicas, hex-cut, amber, black-lined with rainbow luster #89C (medium/M)
8-10g Size 8 Delicas, hex-cut, clear, blue-lined luster #58C (light/L)
8-10g Size 10 Delicas, clear, blue-lined luster #58 (light/L)
8-10g Size 11 Delicas, clear, blue-lined luster #58 (light/L)
16 Wooden beads, 10mm
5 Wooden beads, 12mm
Silver acrylic paint
Toothpicks
K-O beading thread, brown or gray or Nymo B
Beading needles, size 10 and 12
54 Potato pearls, 4mm, light beige/gray
20 Rice pearls, 4 x 6mm, dark peacock or dark gray-green
28" (72cm) Flexible beading wire, size .014-.018
2 Sterling silver tube crimp beads, 2 x 2mm
2 Sterling silver crimp covers, optional
1 Sterling silver box clasp with mystic topaz, PacificSilverworks.com
Crimping pliers
Bead design board, optional

How-to

Before beginning to bead, paint the wooden beads silver. I do this by putting them in a small cup of aluminum foil, squirting acrylic paint onto them, and rolling them in the paint with a toothpick until they are completely covered. I place each bead on a toothpick and insert the other end into the corrugations on the edge of a cut corrugated box until the paint is dry.

I made five large bicone beads (the only size that uses 12mm wooden beads), eight small bicones (four of which are more angled because the center row beads are pearls), and eight small round beads. The figures for the bead patterns are shown flat. Refer to the directions for tubular herringbone stitch with a ladder base in Basic Techniques on page 6.

All of the beads feature herringbone increasing and decreasing. I've given a color pattern for each bead, but use your own imagination for additional beads.

Large Bicone Bead (make 5)

Thread the needle with about 5 ft. (1.5m) of thread.

Row 1 (yellow): Make a ladder with 8 size 11L (light) and join it into a ring (see "Brick stitch," figures 1 and 2, in Basic Techniques).

Row 2 (wheat): Work 4 stitches of tubular herringbone with size 11L.

Row 3 (light orange): Step up and repeat row 2.

Row 4 (orange): Begin the increase by inserting 1 size 10M between each new 11L stitch.

Row 5 (red): Complete the increase by inserting 2 size 10M between each 11L stitch.

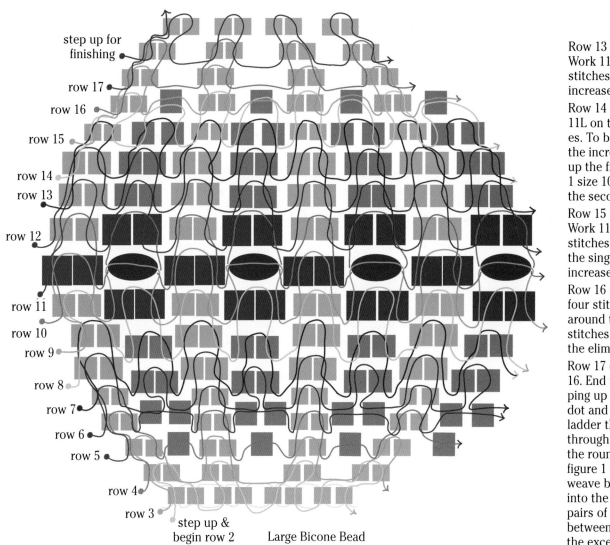

step up for finishing

row 17
row 16
row 15
row 14
row 13
row 12
row 11
row 10
row 9
row 8
row 7
row 6
row 5
row 4
row 3

step up & begin row 2

Large Bicone Bead

Row 13 (dark burgundy): Work 11L on the original stitches and 10M on the increase stitches.

Row 14 (wheat): Work 11L on the original stitches. To begin eliminating the increase stitches, sew up the first 10M, pick up 1 size 10M and sew down the second 10M.

Row 15 (light orange): Work 11L on the original stitches and sew through the single bead on the increase stitches.

Row 16 (orange): Work four stitches of 11L around the row. Pull the stitches together over the eliminated increases.

Row 17 (red): Repeat row 16. End the bead by stepping up (top burgundy dot and line) to work a ladder thread path through the 8 beads of the round as shown in figure 1 on page 11. Then weave both thread tails into the bead tying 2-3 pairs of half hitches between beads. Cut off the excess threads.

Row 6 (burgundy): Work 10L on the original stitches and work regular herringbone stitches using 10M on the increase pairs (there are now 8 regular stitches).

Row 7 (dark burgundy): Repeat row 6.

Row 8 (wheat): Work 10L on the original stitches and size 8D on the increase stitches.

Row 9 (light orange): Work 8D on the original stitches. On the increase stitches work as follows: Come up the first bead, pick up a rice pearl, and sew down the second bead. Adjust the thread tension so the pearl holes are horizontal.

Row 10 (orange): Work 10L on the original stitches. Over the pearls, sew front to back through the thread at the beginning of the pearl. Pick up 2 size 8D and sew from the back to the front through the thread at the end of the pearl.

Row 11 (red): Work 10L on the original stitches. Sew through the first 8D over the pearl, pick up 2 size 10M and sew through the second 8D. Insert a 12mm wooden bead after stepping up at the end of this row.

Row 12 (burgundy): Work 10L on the original stitches and 10M on the increase stitches.

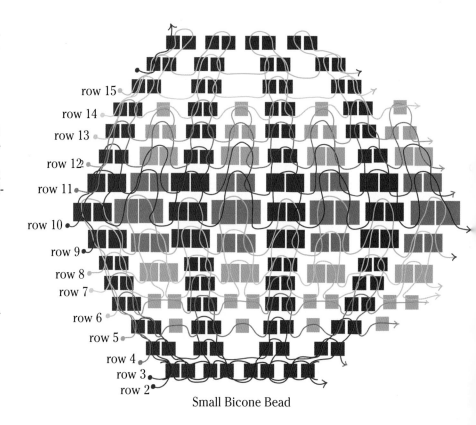

row 15
row 14
row 13
row 12
row 11
row 10
row 9
row 8
row 7
row 6
row 5
row 4
row 3
row 2

Small Bicone Bead

Small Bicone Bead (make 4)

Thread the needle with about 4 ft. (1.2m) of thread.

Row 1 (dark burgundy): Make a ladder with 8 size 11D (dark) and join it into a ring.

Row 2 (burgundy): Work 4 stitches of tubular herringbone with size 11D.

Row 3 (red): Repeat row 2.

Row 4 (orange): Begin the increase by inserting 1 size 11L between each 11D stitch.

Row 5 (light orange): Complete the increase by inserting 2 size 11L between each 11D stitch.

Row 6 (wheat): Work 11D on the original stitches and work regular herringbone stitches using 10L on the increase pairs (there are now 8 regular stitches).

Row 7 (yellow-green): Work 10D on the original stitches and 10M on the increase stitches.

Row 8 (green): Work 10D on the original stitches and 8M on the increase stitches.

Row 9 (burgundy): Repeat row 7. Insert a 10mm wooden bead.

Row 10 (red): Repeat row 6.

Row 11 (orange): Work 11D on the original stitches and 11L on the increase stitches.

Row 12 (light orange): Work 11D on the original stitches. To begin eliminating the increases, sew up the first 11L of the increase stitch, pick up a single 11L and sew down the second 11L of the increase stitch.

Row 13 (wheat): Work 11D on the original stitches and sew through the single bead on the increase stitches.

Row 14 (yellow-green): Work four stitches of 11D around the row. Pull the stitches together over the eliminated increases.

Row 15 (green): Repeat row 14. End the bead by stepping up (top burgundy dot and line) to work a ladder thread path through the 8 beads of the round as shown in figure 1. Then weave both thread tails into the bead tying 2-3 pairs of half hitches between beads. Cut off the excess threads.

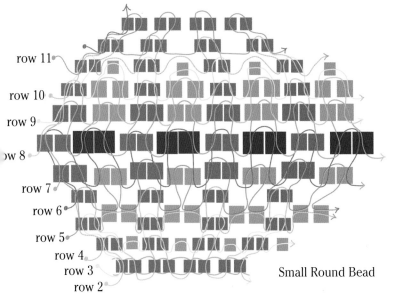

row 11
row 10
row 9
ow 8
row 7
row 6
row 5
row 4
row 3
row 2

Small Round Bead

Pearl Bicone Bead (make 4)

Rows 1-7: Work like the small bicone.

Row 8: Work the original stitches as you did on row 7. Pick up 2 potato pearls instead of 2 size 8 Delicas on the increase stitches.

Rows 9-15: Work like the small bicone. (On row 9, stitch through the pearls as you would for a normal herringbone stitch.)

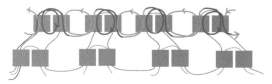

Figure 1

Small Round Bead (make 8)

The wooden bead fits tightly inside this beaded covering. Start with 1 yd. (.9m) of thread.

Row 1 (green): Make a ladder with 8 size 11M (medium) and join it into a ring.

Row 2 (yellow-green): Work 4 stitches of tubular herringbone with size 11M.

Row 3 (yellow): Begin the increase by inserting 1 size 11L between each 11M stitch.

Row 4 (wheat): Complete the increase by inserting 2 size 10L between each 11M stitch.

Row 5 (light orange): Work 10M on the original stitches and work regular herringbone stitches using 10L on the increase pairs (there are now 8 regular stitches).

Row 6 (orange): Work 10M on the original stitches and 8D on the increase stitches.

Row 7 (green): Work like round 5.

Row 8 (yellow-green): Work 11M on the original stitches and 10L on the increase stitches. Insert the 10mm wooden bead.

Row 9 (yellow): Work 11M on the original stitches. To begin eliminating the increases, sew up the first 10L of the increase stitch, pick up a single 11L and sew down the second 10L of the increase stitch.

Row 10 (wheat): Work the 4 original stitches with 11M. Do not sew through the single beads on the increase stitches when you get to them. Thread will show between the stitches but it will be below the level of the beads and almost invisible.

Row 11 (light orange): Work the 4 original stitches with 11M, pulling them tightly together. End the bead by stepping up (top orange dot and line) to work a ladder thread path through the 8 beads of the round as shown in figure 1. Then weave both thread tails into the bead tying 2-3 pairs of half hitches between beads. Cut off the excess threads.

Stringing the Necklace

1. I placed a potato pearl between each beaded bead.

The beaded beads are organized as follows: round, small bicone, round, pearl bicone, round, large bicone, small bicone, round, large bicone, and pearl bicone. A large bicone goes at the center. Then reverse the stringing pattern to the other end.

2. When you like the position of each of the beads, string them on flexible beading wire. At each end of the strand, string a potato pearl, a crimp tube, and a dark size 10 Delica.

3. Thread one end of the wire through the loop at one end of the clasp and pass it back through the Delica, the crimp, and the pearl if possible. Close the crimp securely with crimping pliers. If desired, cover it with a crimp cover.

4. Tighten the beads on the strand, leaving a tiny bit of slack so the necklace will hang gracefully, and repeat step 3 on the other clasp loop. Clip the excess beading wire as close to the bead it exits as possible.

Braided Crystal Bracelet

I loved Girl Scouts. That's where I learned to make this easy flat four-strand braid. I also love working tubular Ndebele herringbone – especially the twisted version. For this bracelet, I've increased the amount of twist by working the twist stitch on every stitch of each tube.

You may find starting the beadwork a bit tricky since you work a large plain tube at the start that you then subdivide into four twisted tubes. After braiding, you end the beadwork by reuniting the four tubes into one large-diameter tube again.

Make your finished bracelet less than 1/2" (1.3cm) larger than your wrist so the jeweled clasp will stay on top.

Materials
20g Size 10/0 Delica beads, aquamarine luster, #179 (dark)
10g each Size 10/0 Delica beads: seafoam luster, #84 (medium), and light aqua luster, #83 (light)
7g Size 15/0 Miyuki seed beads, black AB, #455
1 Sterling silver slide clasp, 5-loop, 31mm long
Beading thread, K-O green or Nymo B
Beading needles, size 12 or 13
12 Swarovski bicone crystals, 4mm, light sapphire champagne
8 Swarovski bicone crystals, 4mm, aquamarine satin
30 Swarovski bicone crystals, 3mm, light sapphire champagne

How-to
The bracelet consists of four twisted herringbone tubes, each having three stitches.

Weaving the Tubes

1. Start by weaving a ladder of 24 beads in the following pattern (see figure 1, p. 5 in "Brick stitch" Basic Techniques): 2D (dark), 4M (medium), 2L (light), 6D, 4L, 2M, and 4D. There should be 24 beads. Do not reinforce the ladder. Leave a 24" long (61cm) starting thread tail.

2. Make sure the ladder is not twisted and join it into a ring by sewing through the first bead then the last bead and finally the first bead again (photo 1 and figure 2 in "Brick stitch" Basic Techniques).

3. Work 3 rounds of tubular Ndebele herringbone (see figure 1, p. 6, "Tubular Ndebele Herringbone," Basic Techniques), following the color pattern of the ladder. Check the fit of the tube over the loops on one side of the clasp and fold it so that at one end there are 1¹/₂ dark stitches on each side and the thread exits one of these stitches (photo 2).

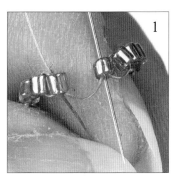
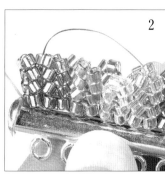

4. Immediately begin twisted herringbone with the end group of 3 dark stitches: Pick up 1D, a 15/0, and a D. Sew down 2 beads on the first stitch and up just the top bead of the next stitch (photo 3).

5. Repeat the stitch pattern in step 4 on all three stitches of the tube. When you get to the end of the first twisted round, step up only through the top bead of the first stitch. A little thread will show for the first round or two (photo 4).

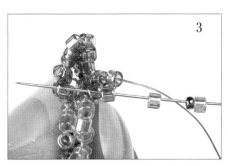
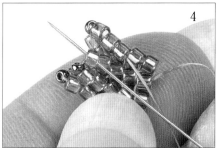

Make the twisted tube about 30 percent longer than the desired length of the finished bracelet. For example, if you want a 7" (17.8cm) bracelet, multiply 7 by 1.3, to get a length of 9" or 23cm. Do not end the thread or tie it off; leave it in place. You may have to add or remove a few rows later.

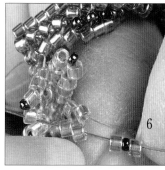

6. To begin the medium-color tube, weave a long thread into the 4-row base so that it exits the top bead on the first medium-color stitch. When you attach the thread, be careful to position it so you will be sewing around the medium-color tube in the same direction as the dark tube. If you go around in the other direction, the tubes will spiral in opposite directions.

One stitch of the medium-color tube will be on one side of the base, and the other two will be on the other side (photo 5). Work the first twisted round snugly to avoid gaps where you change sides on the base (photo 6). After the first round, work this twisted tube just like the first one.

7. Work the light-colored tube, then the final dark-colored tube the same way.

8. Thread a needle on the starting thread tail and slip the ladder base rows over the loops on one of the clasp parts, positioning the tube so there is one dark stitch on one side of the loops and two on the other side. Work the thread through beads so it exits the bottom of the first herringbone row, rather than the edge of the ladder, and sew through the beadwork and the first clasp loop, then out the other side of the base at the bottom of the first herringbone row (photo 7). Reposition the needle on the second side so you can sew back through the loop and first side in the space between the top of the ladder and the bottom of the first row. Repeat several times.

9. Work the needle through the beads on whichever side you are to reach the second loop and repeat the process to attach both sides to each loop between the ladder and the first herringbone row (photo 8).

Braiding the Bracelet

1. Lay the bracelet out flat. Cross the bottom tube under the third tube, over the second, and under the first at a slight angle (photo 9).

2. The bottom tube is now at the top. Straighten it and line it up with the tube below it. Weave the now bottom tube up to the top, going under, over, then under the other three tubes (photo 10).

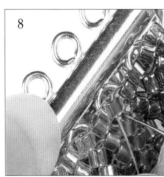

3. As you work, keep straightening the braid so it doesn't angle away from the line of the clasp and keep the braiding tension firm and even.

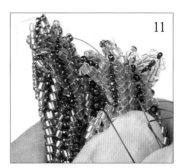

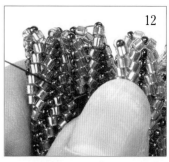

4. The ends of the tubes will be uneven when you finish braiding. Use a contrasting color thread to baste the last braid cross in place (photo 11). Then measure the bracelet around your wrist and lengthen or shorten each tube as needed for the desired fit.

5. You may have to unbraid, then rebraid the bracelet. When the braided portion is the right length and the end is basted, remove stitches on the too-long tubes until they are all the same length.

6. If the thread on one of the end tubes is at least 24" (61cm) long, you can use it to work the end of the bracelet. Weave and knot the other 3 threads into their tubes to end them. If necessary, end all 4 threads and start a new thread to exit the end of one of the tubes.

7. Hold the 4 tubes next to each other and flat. They should alternately present 2 stitches on one side and one on the other (photo 12).

8. Work a round of plain, untwisted herringbone around all the stitches following their color pattern: two stitches of tube 1, one stitch of tube 2, two stitches of tube 3, and all three stitches of tube 4, then one of tube 3, two of tube 2, and one of tube 1. You will have to twist some of the stitches slightly to position the correct number of stitches on each side of the large single tube (photo 13).

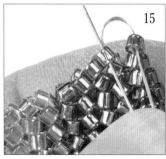

9. Work a total of 4 rounds of herringbone to complete this end of the bracelet (photo 14).

10. Finally, work around the last round again in the ladder thread pattern to firm the end of the tube (photo 15 and figure 1 in "Beaded Gems," p. 11). Remove the basting stitches.

11. Close the clasp and begin to join the final end to the second part just as you joined the first end. After attaching the first loop, you can open the clasp to make sewing easier.

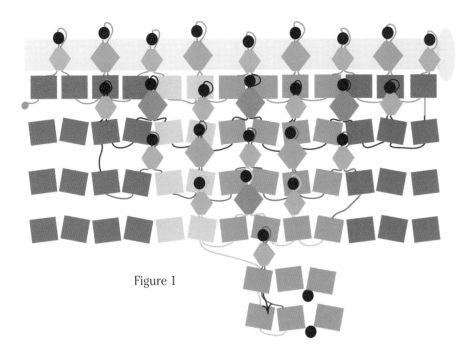

Figure 1

Adding the Crystal Trim

1. Weave a new doubled thread that is at least 30" (76cm) long into the beadwork at one end of the bracelet, exiting the edge bead of the ladder toward the clasp.

2. String a 3mm crystal and a seed bead. Sew back down the crystal and back into the next ladder bead (see figure 1).

3. Sew out the next bead on the ladder (#3) and string a 4mm light sapphire champagne crystal and a seed bead. Sew back down the crystal and into the same ladder bead (#3).

4. Sew out the next ladder bead (#4) and string a 3mm crystal and a seed bead. Sew back down the crystal and into the next ladder bead (photo 16).

5. Repeat steps 3 and 4 until you've attached five 3mm crystals and four 4mm crystals. The last 3mm crystal will attach to the 13th ladder bead and will slightly overlap the edge. Sew back down the same bead (figure 1, top right).

6. Reposition your needle so you are exiting the row 2 bead in line with the end 4mm crystal and are pointing toward the clasp. Begin row 2 with a 3mm crystal and sew back into the same bead you exited. Sew out the next bead and place a 4mm aquamarine satin crystal. Sew into the third bead. On this row, the 3mm crystals go into and come out the same herringbone beads and the 4mm crystals span 2 beads. Alternate a total of four 3mm crystals and three 4mm crystals.

7. For row 3, bring the needle out the first bead on the next row below the end 4mm crystal. Attach a 3mm crystal to 2 beads as you did on row 1. Alternate three 3mm crystals with two 4mm light sapphire champagne crystals sewn as in row 1.

8. Reposition your needle in row 4 as shown in the figure. Alternate two 3mm crystals attached as in step 6 with one 4mm aquamarine satin crystal.

9. Finish up with a fifth row of a 3mm crystal attached to the bead below the 4mm crystal on row 4 (photo 17).

10. Close the clasp to make sure that you attach the first 3mm crystal on the second side perfectly aligned with its mate on the first side. Then open the clasp to repeat the crystal pattern.

Frilled Cuff

The idea to enhance a simple peyote tube with a lavish ruffle came to me in the shower. Covering a bargain bangle with tubular peyote stitch is easy and goes quickly – especially with size 10 Delicas.

Then take advantage of the size differential between size 11 and 10 Delicas to make an easy peyote ruffle with only one round of increasing.

Materials

20g Size 10 Delicas, crimson luster, #105
22-25g Size 10 Delicas, hematite, #1
15g Size 11 Delicas, nickel-plated antique silver, #21
7g Miyuki seed beads, size 11/0, black, #10
7-10g Miyuki seed beads, size 15/0, antique silver, #190
K-O beading threads: red, black, pale gray or Nymo B
Narrow bangle bracelet that's a bit loose (try a thrift store)
    or 3-5 soldered wire bangles (Darice, in a crafts store)
Beading needles, size 12

How-to

Cover your bangle with tubular peyote stitch. Then sew beads along the outer circumference to serve as the base for a peyote ruffle. Work as many rows of ruffle as you wish and end with a two-row edging.

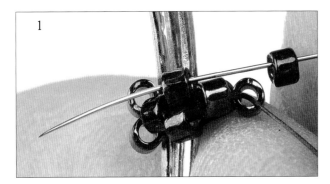

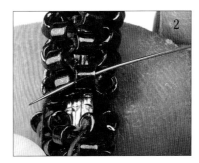

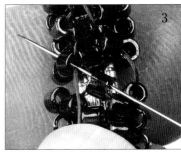

Covering the Bangle

1. If you use Darice soldered wire bangles as I did, hold 3-5 of them together to create a thick enough core.

2. Using red thread, String 8 size 10 Delicas and join them into a ring around the bangle by sewing through all of them a second time. (If your bangle is thicker, you may need more beads in the starting circle, but string an even number.) Leave a 4-6" (10-15cm) thread tail to weave in later.

3. Begin even-count tubular peyote as shown in "Peyote stitch," figure 1, p. 7, in Basic Techniques and photo 1. Pick up a red bead, skip the next red bead on the ring and sew through the third. Repeat around.

4. When you have picked up the fourth bead, you will need to step up. Go through the bead you went through before picking up the first bead and continue through the first new bead.

5. Work around the bangle, stepping up each time you've picked up the fourth bead for the round, until the skin of beads covers the bangles and the ends almost meet.

6. You will need to add thread as you work. Do not end the old thread until you've added the new thread and worked several rounds.

To add thread, start weaving the new thread into the beadwork on crossing diagonals several rows below the end of your work. End by bringing the new thread through the same bead the old thread exits.

End the old thread the same way by weaving it through the beadwork on several crossing diagonals. If you wish, you can tie a few double half hitches between beads as you weave in the new and old threads for added security (see "Knots" in Basic Techniques).

7. Adjust the tube of beads so it is not twisted and the same line of beads is along the outer circumference.

8. The working thread is going through a recessed "down" bead at the end of the tube. Go through the next bead, which sticks "up" slightly. Sew through the matching extended "up" bead on the starting end (photo 2).

9. Continue sewing back and forth alternating "up" beads on the ends of the tube to graft the ends together seamlessly (photo 3). Repeat the thread path. Then end the working and starting thread tails in the beadwork.

Beginning the Ruffle

1. Weave a new, black thread as long as you can manage comfortably into the beadwork. Exit a bead on the outside circumference. Work with dark silver size 11 Delicas.

2. Round 1 – Pick up a silver bead (light gray on figure 1) and sew through the next red bead in line with the one you exited, going in the other direction (blue line). Pick up another bead and go through the third bead on the row in the same direction as the first bead (photo 4). Continue adding a bead between each bead on the circumference row until you get back to the first bead and go through the first red size 10 and the first silver size 11 (figure 1, blue to medium blue line).

Note: If your tube was a bit twisted when you joined the ends, you will have to add a bead between 2 circumference beads, working on the diagonal, so that you end where you began.

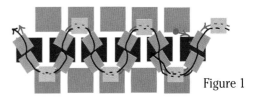

Figure 1

3. Round 2 – Pick up 2 silver beads (darker gray on figure 1) between each of the beads you added in round 1 (photo 5). End by going through the first silver bead of the previous round and the first bead added on this round, a step up (figure 1, purple to royal blue line).

4. Thread a scrap piece of thread through a bead on the band next to the ruffle step up and tie its ends together. Although the step up moves one bead per round in the direction you're working, the thread will alert you to the fact that you are nearing the end of a round (photo 7).

Figure 2

5. Round 3 – The first peyote row of the ruffle alternates a regular stitch with an increase: Pick up an 11 Delica (figur 2, darker than the round 2 beads) and go through the second bead of the first pair. Pick up 2 beads and go through the first bead of the second pair. Repeat around (photo 6 and figure 2, blue dot and line). End by stepping up through the first silver bead added in round 2 and the first bead added on this round (magenta line).

The round will look extremely crowded with zigzags of silver Delicas, but it is the only increase round in the ruffle. Additional increasing is caused by adding progressively more size 10 beads and fewer size 11 beads per round.

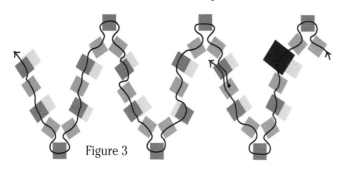

Figure 3

6. Round 4 – Add mostly size 11 silver Delicas on this round (shown darker than the beads of rounds 2 and 3), but every couple of inches (5cm) or so add a red size 10 in order to bring the band color into the ruffle (I added 12 red beads on this round). With your needle exiting the first bead of round 3 (a single bead), pick up a bead and go through the first bead of the increase pair. Pick up a bead and go through the second bead of the increase pair. Pick up a bead and go through the next single bead. Repeat around, stepping up through the first bead of round 3, then the first bead of this round (figure 3, magenta dot and line to blue line).

Working the Ruffle

1. Round 5 – This is the first round that looks like normal peyote stitch with alternating "up" and "down" beads. Use mostly silver beads, but add a red 10 before and after going through each red bead on the previous round (add 2 red beads per section).

2. Round 6 – Add 3 reds in each red section and roughly center 1 hematite size 10 Delica in one or two places between the red bead sections. Add 2 spaced out hematite beads only if the gap between red beads is especially large.

3. Rounds 7 and following – Continue adding one more size 10 Delica in each color section than you added on the previous round. Don't forget to step up when you get to the end of the round where 2 beads are next to each other in a shallow diagonal (photo 7).

4. Round 9 – Start transitioning to all hematite by adding 1 hematite size 10 near the center of each red section.

5. When a red and a hematite section meet, continue increasing the width of the hematite section as you decrease the width of the red section. Continue in this manner until you have worked at least one round of all hematite size 10 Delicas (in my case, a total of 16 rounds).

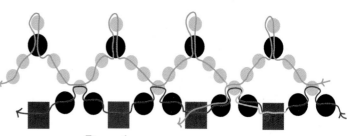

Figure 4

Working the Edging

1. Coming through the first peyote stitch bead on the last round (figure 4, red dot), pick up a black, size 11/0 seed bead, a silver size 15/0, and a black size 11/0. Go through the next peyote bead and repeat around (figure 4, red line).

2. Step up at the end of the first edging round by going through the first peyote bead and the first 2 beads of the first edging stitch (figure 4, yellow line).

3. For the second and final edging round, with the needle exiting a 15/0 on the previous round, pick up 2 size 15/0s, a black 11/0, and a 15/0.

Sew down the black bead and tighten the stitch. Pick up 2 size 15/0s and go through the next 15/0 on the previous round (figure 4, goldenrod line).

4. End by sewing through the 15/0 from which you began round 2. Then weave and knot the thread securely into the beadwork.

Lotus Necklace

When I began planning the projects for this book, the idea of making a lotus with graduated Delicas in layers was one of the first that came to me. Of course, my original concept didn't work. But that was a blessing in disguise because these flowers are much prettier than my first idea would have been.

Since this necklace is a bit over the top – you might want to wear it for your next red-carpet appearance or the opening gala at the opera (although I'll probably wear mine over a turtleneck with a jeans skirt) – I splurged and bought real pearls for the centers of the lotuses and the necklace strands. You could, however, substitute glass pearls.

The necklace should fit like a choker at or just below the hollow in your throat. Mine has eight lotuses, which reach all the way around to my shoulders.

Materials

50g Size 8 Delicas, metallic gold-plated #34
20g Size 10 Delicas, hex-cut dusty rose luster #103C
10g Size 11 Delicas, pastel pink #106
K-O beading thread, red, gold or brown, and pink or Nymo B (you could use size D with the gold beads)
Beading needles, size 12 or 13
1 Strand (16" / 41cm) round freshwater pearls, 10-11mm (from KnotJustBeads.com)
1 Strand (16" / 41cm) nearly round freshwater pearls, 7-8mm (from KnotJustBeads.com)
18-22 Vermeil barrel beads, mine are 9 x 14mm
Stringth or Pearlsilk beading cord, size 1 or 2
Twisted wire beading needles
French wire (bullion wire), gold
Heavy bronze clasp (mine is from Ashes2Beauty.com)
G-S Hypo Cement
Awl or favorite pearl knotting tool, optional

How-to

Start with the middle layer of the flower to make the brick stitch base ring. Then work the inner petal layer off the beads at the center of the ring. Next complete the petals on the outer edge of the base. Finally appliqué a ring of the largest beads to the back of the base and work the outer layer of petals. When you have completed 7-9 lotuses, you are ready to string the necklace.

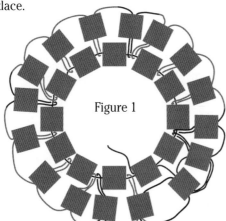

Figure 1

Making the Base

1. Thread a needle with 2 yd. (1.8m) of red thread. String 12 size 10 beads and sew through them again twice to form a snug ring.

2. With the needle exiting any bead, pick up 2 and sew under the thread after the next ring bead to work the starting brick stitch (see "Brick stitch" figure 3, p. 5 in Basic Techniques and figure 1, above).

3. Increase by sewing the third bead to the same space.

4. Add a brick-stitch bead to the thread after the next ring bead. Repeat twice more.

5. Increase by adding the seventh bead to the same space as the sixth.

6. Repeat steps 4 and 5 twice more.

7. End by adding a bead to the last space. Then join the round by sewing down the first bead and back up the last bead. There will be 16 beads in the first round.

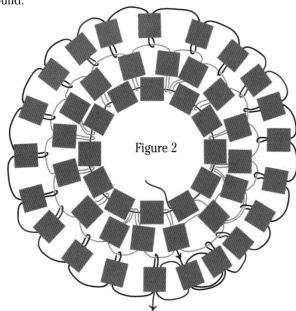

Figure 2

8. To begin the next round of the base (figure 2, dot at bottom), repeat steps 2 and 3.

9. Add 1 bead in each of the next 4 spaces. Then increase in the same space as the last bead. Repeat twice more.

10. Add 1 bead in each of the remaining 3 spaces. Join the round as in step 7. There will be 21 beads in this round. Remove the needle, but leave the long red thread in place to work the second layer.

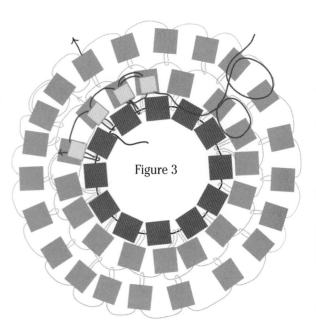

Figure 3

First Layer of Petals

Use size 11 Delicas for the first layer.

1. Thread a needle with 1 yd. (.9m) of pink thread. Weave it into the base securely (figure 3, purple line) and come out a center ring bead about 2 beads to the right of the long red thread (figure 3).

2. Work 4 brick stitches off the threads between the ring beads. Add the first pair of beads to the first thread loop after the ring bead you have gone through. Then add the next 2 beads to the next 2 threads.

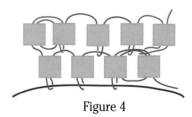

Figure 4

3. Increase at the beginning of the second row by attaching the first 2 beads to the first thread loop. After adding the fourth bead to the last thread loop, increase again by adding the fifth bead to the same loop as the fourth (figure 4, left to right).

4. Work an increase at the beginning and end of the next 2 rows to reach a width of 7 beads.

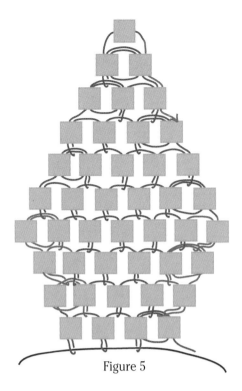

Figure 5

5. Now work normal brick stitch to taper the petal to a point of 1 bead as shown in figure 5 and the Basic Technique.

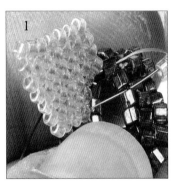

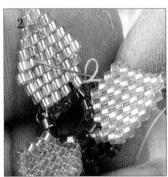

6. Sew down the side edge beads of the petal to the ring (blue line at top right). Go through 1 ring bead and repeat steps 2-5 (photo 1).

7. Repeat step 6 to make the third petal and secure the thread in the base ring with a pair of half hitch knots (photo 2).

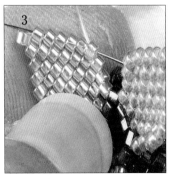

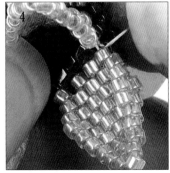

8. Sew up the beads on the side of the closest petal, through the top bead, and down the beads on the other side of the petal (photo 3).

9. Pull the thread to gather the edge of the petal so it cups (photo 4). Secure the gathers at the base of the petal with a pair of half hitch knots.

10. Repeat steps 8-9 to cup the other 2 petals. Then end the thread securely in the last petal.

Middle Layer of Petals

1. Thread a needle on the long red thread. Work a row of 7 beads, making the first stitch of 2 beads in the thread loop after the bead your needle is exiting (photo 5). The row of beads should be centered on the space between 2 pink petals.

2. Work the next 2 rows increasing at each edge as in step 3 of the first layer. The third row will have 9 beads.

3. Work regular brick stitch to a point of 1 bead.

4. Sew down the edge of the finished petal and into the edge bead on the 21-bead base row. Sew out the next bead on the base to begin the second petal (photo 6). Work it like the first.

5. Repeat step 4 to work the third petal. End by sewing down the base row bead.

6. Sew up the next base bead and the first 2 edge beads of the first petal. Tie a pair of half hitches so you won't gather the increasing rows, only the tapered rows of the middle-layer petals (photo 7).

7. Sew through the edge beads from the first side of the widest row to the bead at the other end of this row. Pull the thread to make the point of the petal cup and secure the gather with a pair of half hitches below the bead at the edge of the widest row.

8. Sew down the next 2 rows, through the base and up the base and first 2 rows of the next petal (photo 8). Knot as in step 6 and repeat step 7 to gather the second petal.

9. Repeat step 8 to gather the third petal. Then end the thread securely in the petal.

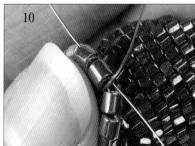

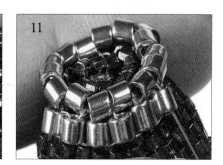

Outer Layer of Petals

Use size 8 Delicas for this layer. Work tightly so the petals stay shapely.

1. Thread a needle with $2^{1/2}$ yds. (2.3m) of gold or brown thread (size B or D). String 15 beads and go through them once. Tie the working thread and tail together with a surgeon's knot to form a tight ring. Go through the ring again.

2. Place the gold ring against the base and sew from top to bottom through the nearest bead on the 16-bead row of the base. Carry the needle under the gold ring's thread (photo 9).

3. Bring the thread up to the front of the gold ring and sew through the next 2 beads (photo 10).

4. Repeat steps 2 and 3 to anchor the gold ring to the 16-bead row of the base.

5. Sew through the ring to exit a bead that's lined up with the center of a rose-colored petal.

6. On row 1, you will add 6 gold beads to 4 spaces between ring beads (photo 11). You may have to vary the increase patterns given below to get the smoothest results:

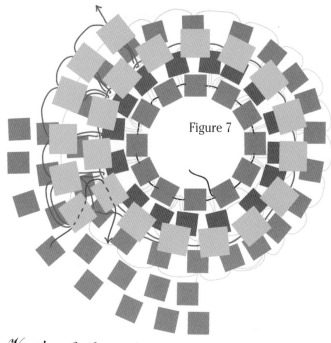

Figure 7

Version 2 (figure 7):

a. Attach 2 beads to the first space.

b. Attach 1 bead to the second space.

c. Attach 2 beads, one at a time, to the third space.

d. Attach 1 bead to the fourth space.

7. For the next 2 rows of brick stitch, increase at the beginning and end to a total of 8 beads.

8. Work normal tapered brick stitch to a 1-bead point.

9. Sew down the edge of the first petal and through the ring bead below the first stitch (figure 7, blue line) to begin the second petal (photo 12), working it like the first.

10. Because the widest row of the petal has an even number of beads, you will have to sew diagonally down the second petal through the beads one in from the edge to get to the place where you begin the third petal. When you sew through the second row, you will be at the edge (photo 13). Continue down the first edge bead and repeat step 9.

11. Then gather the petals between the widest rows as on the second layer.

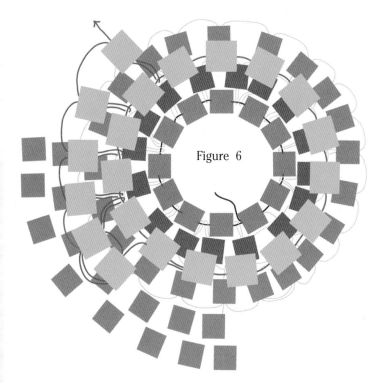

Figure 6

Version 1 (figure 6):

a. Attach 2 beads to the first space. Attach the third bead to the same space.

b. Attach 1 bead to each of the next 3 spaces.

Stringing the Necklace

You must string two strands to keep the lotuses upright.

1. For the first strand, cut a length of beading cord 5 times the desired length of the necklace and thread a twisted wire needle to the center of the cord so it is doubled.

2. Tie a stop bead about 6" (15cm) from the end of the tails.

3. For the end of the strand, string a vermeil bead and a size 10 Delica. Make the first pearl knot (if desired). String a 10mm pearl, knot, and a size 10. Repeat the pattern. End with a vermeil bead, a 10, and 2 size 8 Delicas.

4. Sew up through the center of a lotus and string a 10mm pearl. Sew back down the lotus. As you tighten the thread, position the pearl so its hole is horizontal and doesn't show (photo 14).

5. Between lotuses, string 2 size 8s, a 10, a vermeil bead, and a 10.* Make sure the cord is snug and knot (photo 15). String a 10mm pearl and knot. Repeat the stringing pattern from the * in reverse.

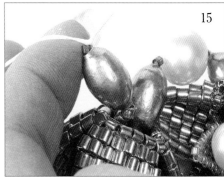

6. Repeat steps 4 and 5 until the strand almost reaches around your neck at the level of a high choker.

7. Repeat step 3 in reverse.

8. Cut a piece of French wire that's 1/2 to 5/8" (1.3-1.6cm) long and carefully thread it onto the needle and down to the beads. Pass the needle through one clasp loop, centering the French wire in the loop.

9. Sew down the end size 10 and tighten the loop of French wire around the clasp loop. You'll have to cut off the needle to tie a front-back-front knot below the bead (see "Knots" in Basic Techniques). Sew both tails through the vermeil bead and tie another front-back-front knot. Sew through the next 10 and tie a final front-back-front knot. If possible, sew one or both tails through the pearl. Before cutting the thread tails off, coat the three knots with G-S Hypo Cement.

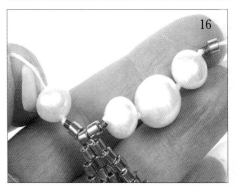

10. Remove the stop bead at the starting end and repeat steps 8 and 9 to attach the other clasp part.

11. Repeat steps 1 and 2 for the second strand. Pick 4 small pearls and 2 large pearls with the largest holes and set half of them aside.

12. String the first set of large-hole pearls, small, large, small and knot after the third pearl.

13. String a size 10 and an 8 and sew through the top size 8 on the top gold petal of the first lotus. You may have to turn the flower slightly to position one petal at the top.

14. String an 8 and a 10, knot, and string a small, large, and small pearl knotting after each (photo 16). Note: Make sure the beads are snug before tying each knot.

15. Repeat steps 13 and 14 until you've sewn through the top of the last lotus.

16. For the end of the strand, string an 8 and a 10 and knot. Then string the reserved 3 large-hole pearls, small, large, small.

17. Repeat step 8. Sew back through the end pearl and tighten the French wire loop. Make a front-back-front knot after the pearl and sew through the middle pearl. Knot again. If possible, sew one or both cord ends through the third pearl. Glue the knots as in step 9.

Repeat this step at the starting end of the strand.

Ripples in the Sand

Odd-count flat peyote with three Delica sizes makes an elegant wave pattern. I planned to make only a bracelet in this design. But as my bracelet strip neared completion, I became entranced by the effect that curving it produced and was compelled to make it into a collar. Large pearls at the bottom edge spread it into the desired curve, and tuck stitches at the top hold the neckline. Of course, a simple peyote-stitch toggle completes the look.

To keep the edges of the bracelet even, I added crystals between each wave at each edge. A simple slide clasp makes the bracelet reversible since the ruched ribbon looks different on each side.

Materials

Bracelet
20-25g Size 8 Delicas, bronze #22
10-15g Size 10 Delicas, trans. root beer, rose luster #170
5g Size 11 Delicas, trans. light amber luster #100
3-5g Miyuki seed beads, size 11/0, trans. root beer, rose luster #257
36-48 Swarovski bicone crystals, padparadscha volcano
2-Hole slide clasp, gold-filled or sterling silver

Necklace
40-50g Size 8 Delicas, bronze metallic luster #29
30-40g Size 10 Delicas, trans. root beer, rose luster #170
10-12g Size 11 Delicas, trans. light amber luster #100
3-5g Size 11 Delicas, hex-cut, amber luster, black-lined #89C
6-7g Miyuki seed beads, size 11/0, trans. root beer, rose luster #257
1 Strand (16" / 41cm) of nearly round pearls to complement beads, 8mm (mine are a bronzy green, from KnotJustBeads.com)
2" (5cm) Sterling silver round wire, 20-gauge, half hard
1/2" (1.3cm) Sterling silver fine cable chain

Both
K-O beading thread, gold or dark brown or Nymo B
Beading needles, sizes 10 and 12 or 13

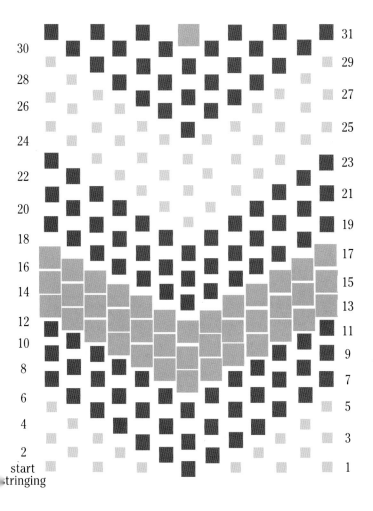

30
28
26
24
22
20
18
16
14
12
10
8
6
4
2
start
stringing

31
29
27
25
23
21
19
17
15
13
11
9
7
5
3
1

a. Keep the tension firm.

b. Change in bead size always begins at the center of the row. When you are changing from size 10 to size 8, pick shorter 8s to fill in over each 10. Then use standard length 8s over established 8s (photo 1).

c. When you reach the full row of 8s, the working edge will appear spread and flat; support it against the side of your finger (photo 2).

d. The chevrons with the smallest beads will fold downward and the chevron pattern will cause the size 8 sections to curve into a raised C-like shape. Pull the tension snug as you add the smaller beads and support the rib of size 8s on the ball of your finger or the side of a fingertip. Keeping the new smaller beads pulled together without gaps is critical to creating the ripple texture (photo 3).

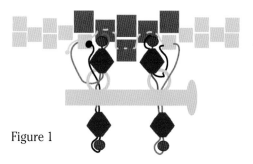

Figure 1

Adding the Clasp and Edging

1. To attach the clasp, work the thread through the first size 11 "up" bead to the right or left of the center on the end row (figure 1, blue dot).

a. Go through the appropriate clasp loop (the left in figure 1) and string a crystal and a seed bead. Go back through the crystal and clasp loop (dark blue line).

b. String a crystal and seed bead on the other side of the loop (blue line).

c. Go back through the crystal and through the size 11 Delica you exited in the same direction that you went through it the first time (orange line).

d. Repeat the thread path at least 3 times.

e. Then weave through the center beads (light green line) to exit the size 11 Delica on the other side of the center and attach it to the other clasp loop the same way. End the thread by weaving it into the bracelet.

2. Close the clasp and remove the stop bead from the starting tail. Thread a needle on the thread and begin to attach the second half of the clasp. Once you have begun attaching it, you can open it to make the process easier.

How-to Bracelet

For a 6" (15cm) bracelet, work a total of 15 pattern repeats in odd-count flat peyote stitch (see "Peyote Stitch," figures 2 and 3, in Basic Techniques on page 7).

Weaving the Band

1. String a small seed bead about 12" (31cm) from the end of a long thread and go through it again for a stop bead (you'll use the tail to attach the clasp.

2. Start stringing on the left-hand edge of the chart, alternating row 1 and 2 beads – 13 beads.

3. Work to row 31 for the starting end and first repeat. Then repeat rows 8-31 for 13 more repeats. End the bracelet with a final repeat, working rows 8-25.

4. Weaving the chevron pattern with different size beads can be tricky. Here are a few tricks for getting the best results:

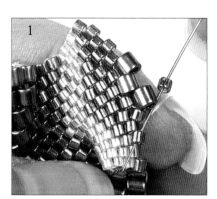

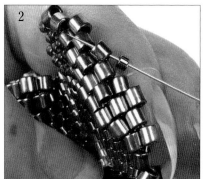

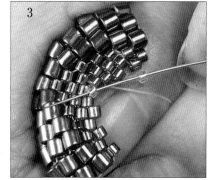

3. To stabilize the edges of the bracelet, weave a doubled thread into it, exiting the third size 8 bead from the edge on the inner side of the first size 8-bead rib with the needle pointing toward the near edge (figure 2, lower light blue line).

4. Pick up a seed bead, a crystal, and a seed bead. Sew into the third size 8 Delica from the edge on the near side of the next rib, sewing away from the near edge (figure 2, first dark blue line).

5. Sew diagonally through the size 8 fourth from the edge. Then sew through the bead next to it toward the edge and come diagonally through the third bead from the edge on the inner side of the rib (figure 2, top light blue line).

6. Repeat steps 4 and 5 until you've joined all the ribs on the first edge. Weave the thread into the beadwork to end it, tying 2-3 pairs of half-hitches between beads.

7. Repeat from step 3, starting with the last size 8 rib to join the ribs on the other edge.

Figure 3

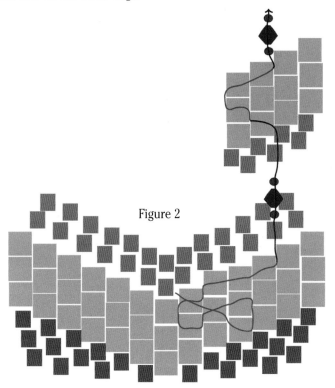

Figure 2

Necklace

1. Repeat steps 1-4 of the bracelet, making a total of 28-32 size 8 Delica ribs (I have 30).

2. Begin the bottom edging at the starting end of the strip with a doubled thread that's about 48" (1.22m) long. Weave the thread into the beadwork, exiting the end size 11 Delica.

3. String an 11/0 seed, an 11 cut Delica, a pearl, a cut, and a seed bead. Sew down the size 10 before the first rib toward the edge (figure 3, lower dark blue line).

4. Work four edging stitches along the bottom edge as follows:

a. Pick up a seed, a cut, and a seed. Sew up the first bottom 8 and diagonally away from the starting end through the second from the edge (figure 3, first medium blue line).

b. Sew down the adjacent 8 and diagonally through the first 8 on the bottom edge. Continue through the last bead of the edging stitch (figure 3, first light blue line).

c. Pick up a cut and a seed and sew into the second 8. Repeat the diagonal crossing pattern to exit the new seed.

d. Make the third edging stitch like the second, but notice the turn through the inner size 10 Delica (figure 3, third medium and light blue lines).

e. Pick up the beads for the fourth edging stitch and go into the first 10 after the rib (figure 3, fourth medium blue line).

5. Repeat steps 3 and 4 (figure 3, top) across the bottom of the necklace, ending with seven edging stitches.

6. To secure the top of the necklace, you pleat the edge of each rib to the size 11 Delicas folded behind it.

7. Weave a new thread into the top of the necklace. Fold the first rib so the first bead is on top, the second 8 is behind it, the third 8 is behind the 10 before it, and the 10s and 11s curve around behind the second layer. Sew through the threads on top of the three layers at the beginning edge of the tuck (photo 4). Reinforce the stitch.

8. As you work toward the edge of the tuck, secure it by sewing around the thread between the edge 8 and 10 and the beads below them. Go through to the back (photo 5). Your needle is at the same level as the edge size 11.

9. Whipstitch around the thread between the 11s and the first 1-2 10s of the next rib.

10. Sew under the edge thread after the first or second 10 to the back, fold the next tuck, and catch it with your needle to begin securing it (photo 6).

11. Repeat to the end. The last 11 is behind end rib.

Making the Toggle Clasp

Feel free to use a purchased clasp if you prefer.

1. For the beaded toggle ring, string 30 size 10 Delicas and sew through them twice to form a secure ring.

2. The beads of the ring make up the first 2 peyote stitch rows. Work around them with 2 more rows of even-count tubular peyote stitch (see "Peyote stitch," figure 1, in Basic Techniques, p. 7, and photo 7).

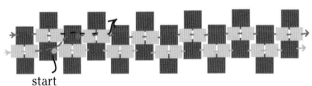

start

Figure 4

3. With your needle coming out a "down" bead on the edge of the ring, pick up 2 size 11 Delicas and sew through the next "down" bead (photo 8). Repeat around to fill the ditch with 11s (figure 4, light blue dot and line).

4. Work over to the nearest "down" bead at the other edge and repeat (figure 4, medium blue line). The ring is becoming stiffer. End by exiting the first pair of 11s added on this row (figure 4, dark blue line).

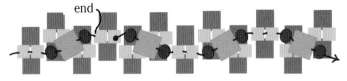

end

Figure 5

5. Now pick up a size 11/0 seed bead, an 8 Delica, and a seed bead. Skip the nearest 11 pair on the other ditch and sew through the next (figure 5, dark blue dot and line). Repeat this process, stitching 3 larger beads diagonally between the ditches. There are ten repeats.

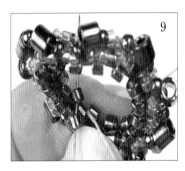

6. Finish the ring, making it strong and stiff, by zipping the "up" beads on rows 1 and 4 of the initial ring together on the inside (photo 9). Repeat the thread path and weave in the shorter thread.

7. Work the remaining thread through the ring to exit one of the seed beads on the outer edge. Pick up a seed and sew through the size 10 Delica at the center of the last row on the ending edge of the necklace. Pick up a seed bead and go through the seed on the adjacent ring trim stitch. Continue through the ditch 11s between the trim stitches and repeat the thread path at least twice more (photo 10).

8. Peyote tube toggle bars tend to be a bit flabby. I wanted my toggle bar to echo the pearl accents on the necklace's bottom edge, so I made it with wire and beads.

9. Unfortunately, pearl holes are too small to accommodate 20-gauge wire, so I used my cordless rotary tool to enlarge the holes of 2 pearls. To do this, wrap the jaws of a pair of loop-closing pliers (their jaws have cup-shaped indentations) with duct tape to hold the hot pearl without scratching it. Insert a broken broach file in the drill chuck (a very thin diamond bit is better) and drill the hole with many stops to let it cool. If it gets too hot, the nacre will burn or crack off the pearl.

10. To make the bar, turn a tiny loop at one end of a 2" (5cm) piece of half-hard sterling silver 20-gauge wire. Press the loop hard with chain-nose pliers to flatten it. String a pearl, seed, Delica 10, 8, seed, 8, and 10. String the end link of a 5/8" to 3/4" (1.6-1.9cm) length of fine cable chain on the wire. Repeat the pattern in reverse. Trim the wire to a little less than 3/8" (1cm) and make another tiny loop in the same plane as the first. Mash it flat, too.

11. Work the starting thread tail of the necklace to the middle size 10 in row 5. Sew through the free end of the chain and the same size 10 (photo 11) 4-6 times, then end the thread in the beadwork.

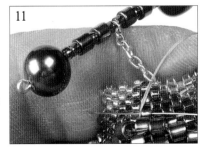

Southwest Sunrise Bracelet

Here's a new way to work twisted tubular herringbone.

I've always loved working twisted tubular herringbone. It's a very relaxing stitch and the result is wonderful. But for these bracelets, I wondered what would happen if I worked the angled twist stitch on every stitch, rather than on only one stitch in the tube. I've also been bothered by the effect of placing the extra, spacer bead in the middle of the twist stitch because it starts so far above the beginning of the tube, so I tried putting it between the stitches. This way it appears at the beginning of the tube. Putting the extra bead here also helps emphasize the twist a little bit more. I also began with an easy, modified version of a herringbone start.

We all tend to be most comfortable beading in one direction rather than the other. Lefties tend to go around a tube counter-clockwise, which produces a leftward twist; while righties tend to bead around a tube clockwise, resulting in a rightward twist. The Southwest Sunrise Bracelet, at top and on page 31, capitalizes on this fact by being formed from two twisted tubes – one worked in each direction. You'll find that the first few rounds in your "wrong" direction are difficult, but pretty soon it will feel like the "right" direction.

Work the gold and crimson bracelet, above, in whatever direction you wish (I chose these colors in memory of my oldest friend, a Harvard grad). I wanted the twisted tube ends to meet, so I used a magnetic clasp with a safety chain, then added crimson focal tubes to conceal the clasp. These short tubes begin in the fourth row from each end.

Materials

Southwest Sunrise and Turquoise Bracelet

14g Miyuki round seed beads, size 8/0, gold-lined clear #195
10-15g Delica size 8, metallic gold iris #23
10-15g Delica size 10, amber luster #170
8-10g Delica size 10, opaque turquoise luster #166
5-7g Miyuki round seed beads, size 15/0, black iris #455
K-O beading thread, yellow or gold or Nymo B
1 Shank button, approx. 5/8" (16mm) diameter, mine is vintage

Crimson and Gold Bracelet

7-10g Miyuki round seed beads, size 8/0, gold-lined clear #195
5-8g Delica size 8, metallic gold #34
5-8g Delica size 10, satin silver-lined dusty rose #191
3-5g Delica size 10, crimson luster #105
3-5g Miyuki round seed beads, size 15/0, salmon-lined clear #275
K-O beading thread, off-white and red or Nymo B
Sterling silver small magnetic clasp
2 Split rings, 4mm
1¹/2" to 2" (3.8-5cm) Sterling silver fine cable chain

Both

Beading needles, size 12 or 13

Figure 1

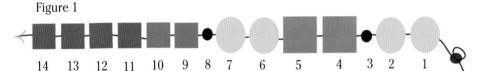

14 13 12 11 10 9 8 7 6 5 4 3 2 1

How-to
Southwest Sunrise Bracelet

Refer to Basic Tecniques on page 6 for the Ndebele or Herringbone technique.

1. Secure a stop bead 14-18" (35-46cm) from the end of as long a thread as you can work with comfortably. Be careful not to split the thread here or in the first 3 rounds. Then string the beads for the first 2 rows as follows: 2 seed 8/0s, a 15/0, 2 Delica size 8s, 2 seed 8/0s, a 15/0, 2 blue size 10s, and 4 amber size 10s (figure 1, purple line to green arrow).

2. Join the beads into a ring by sewing through the first seed 8/0 (figure 2, green line).

3. As you pick up the beads for row 3, tighten the thread to begin pulling them into columns. To begin row 3 (light green line), pick up a 15/0, sew through the second Delica 8 (#5) and pick up 1 Delica 8 and an 8/0 seed.

Sew through the first 8/0 seed strung after the Delica 8s on the starting row (#6). Pick up a 15/0 and sew through the second blue (#10).

Pick up a blue and an amber; sew through the first amber strung after the blues (#11).

Skip the next 2 ambers and sew through the fourth (#14). Then pick up an amber (light green line to dark blue arrow).

Finish the joining stitch by picking up an 8/0 seed and sewing through the first 8/0 seed strung. Tighten the thread again to finish forming definite columns of beads (dark blue line).

4. Work the first step up at the end of row 3 by going through the 15/0 at the beginning of step 3. Sew up only the new Delica 8 (dark blue to blue line).

For row 4, pick up a Delica 8 and an 8/0. Sew down the next 2 size 8/0 seeds and go through the 15/0 added before the blue column.

Sew up only the new blue bead. Pick up a blue and an amber and sew down the next 2 ambers.

begin row 6

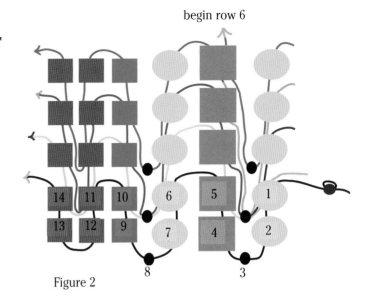

14 11 10 6 5 1
13 12 9 7 4 2
8 3

Figure 2

Sew up only the new amber on the last column and pick up an amber (blue line to orange arrow). Complete the last stitch of row 4 by picking up an 8/0 seed (orange line on right).

5. Join the row and step up to begin row 5 by sewing down the next 2 size 8/0 seeds and the 15/0 picked up at the beginning of step 3. Sew up only the top size 8 Delica (orange line).

To begin row 5 (green line), *pick up an 8 Delica and an 8/0 seed, sew down the 2 size 8/0 seeds below it. Pick up a 15/0 and sew up only the top blue bead.

Pick up a blue and an amber and sew down the 2 ambers below. Sew up only the top amber of the last stitch. Notice that there are no 15/0s between the amber columns.

Pick up an amber and an 8/0 seed and go down the 2 size 8/0 seeds in the first column to complete the row (green line at right).

6. From now on work the normal step up: pick up a 15/0 and sew up only the top Delica 8 on the next column (green line to light green arrow).

7. Repeat from * in step 5 until the tube is long enough.

8. Remove the stop bead and secure the thread tail with 1-2 pairs of half hitches. Bring the thread tail out an end bead.

9. Make a second spiral tube but work around it in the opposite direction. After you've worked 5-6 rows, hold it up next to the first tube. If they both spiral in the same direction, you need to start the second tube over and go the other way.

Calculating Bracelet Length

Since you'll be sewing 2 size 8 Delicas together to join the two tubes the same number of rows apart, row count is important. My 6" (15cm) bracelet is 97 rows long. I've sewn the first 2 and last 2 pairs of 8 Delicas together and have 5 openings with 4 more joinings. To come out even, I've sewn the 18th and 19th beads after the previously joined pair together.

There is some play in this formula. You can add up to 10 rows to the total length by sewing the 20th and 21st beads together to make a bracelet that's about 7" (17.8cm) long without deforming the spirals. (If you add 5 rows, you'll gain nearly $1/2$" (1.3cm) and will sew the 19th and 20th beads together.) For a $7^3/4$" (19cm) bracelet, make 19 more rows (a total of 116 rows) and have 6 openings, following the original joining pattern.

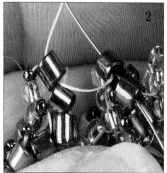

Joining the Tubes

Align the tubes with a starting thread at each end.

1. Secure a new thread in one of the spiral tubes and bring it through the size 8 Delica at the end with the needle pointing toward the other end of the tube.

2. Sew through the end 8 Delica on the other tube toward the near end (photo 1). Then sew down the 8 Delica on the first tube and continue through the next 8 Delica beads (photo 2).

3. Square stitch the second pair of Delicas on the tubes together (figure 3).

Then go through both Delicas on the second tube toward the near end and come back through the first 2 Delicas on the first tube toward the far end (photo 3). Reinforce the join.

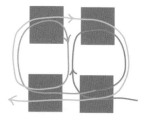

Figure 3

4. Carry the thread through the size 8 Delicas on the first tube, tying half hitches every 2-3 beads so you don't shrink the tube.

5. When you've gone through the 18th bead after the second joining bead, square stitch it to the 18th bead of the second tube, making sure the amount of twist on each tube is the same (photo 4). (Note: see above for joining bead variations to achieve different bracelet lengths.)

6. Square stitch the 19th beads together and reinforce the join.

7. Repeat steps 4-6 until you've joined the last pair of 8 Delicas on the tubes. End the thread securely, but if it's long, leave it in place for the clasp.

8. Thread a needle on the starting thread tail at the beginning end of the bracelet and weave the beads on the end together to gather them into a compact shape (photo 5).

9. You may find it desirable to appliqué some amber size 10 Delicas to the end of the bundle to cover unsightly threads.

10. Use the remaining thread to sew the button to the top of the joined end 2-3 rows in from the end. Then weave in the thread to end it.

11. Repeat steps 8 and 9 at the other end of the bracelet and end the thread.

12. Use either the remainder of the starting tail or the thread left from joining the tubes to sew a loop that will fit over your button onto the end of the bracelet. Reinforce the loop at least 3 times. Then end the thread(s) securely.

Crimson and Gold Bracelet

Use the same pattern chart as for the double bracelet, but substitute crimson for the blue beads, pink for the amber beads, and salmon for the 15/0s. Leave a thread tail of about 12" (30cm) at the beginning of the single tube.

1. When the tube is the desired length, attach a split ring to each clasp part. Sew the split ring inside the tube between beads on opposite sides about three rows below the top row (photo 6).

2. Then sew up to the top beads and sew through them in a ring, catching one end of the safety chain between two beads. You may need to add a size 8 Delica over the columns of size 10 Delicas to level the end (photo 7). Go through the ring twice more.

3. Work the thread tail at the beginning of the tube down about 3 rows and attach the other clasp part inside the tube like the first. Repeat step 2, catching the other end of the safety chain between beads. End this thread securely.

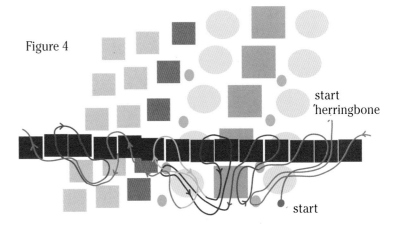

Figure 4

start
'herringbone

start

4. Weave a new red thread into the tube, coming out a bead 4-5 rows from the end. Attach pairs of crimson beads to beads at the same level around the tube (figure 4). You will need 7 pairs of crimson beads and you may have to experiment with this step to space them level and as evenly as possible (photo 8). Use figure 4 only as a guide.

5. Work 7 stitches of plain tubular herringbone off the crimson beads around the end of the tube (photo 9).

6. When you get to the level of the safety chain, bring it to the outside between crimson stitches and keep working until the crimson tube is level with the top surface of the clasp.

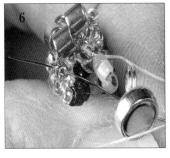

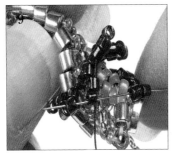

7. End by ladder-stitching the last row of crimson beads together as shown in figure 1 of "Beaded Gems," p. 11, and photo 10. End the thread securely.

8. Repeat steps 4-7 at the other end of the bracelet.

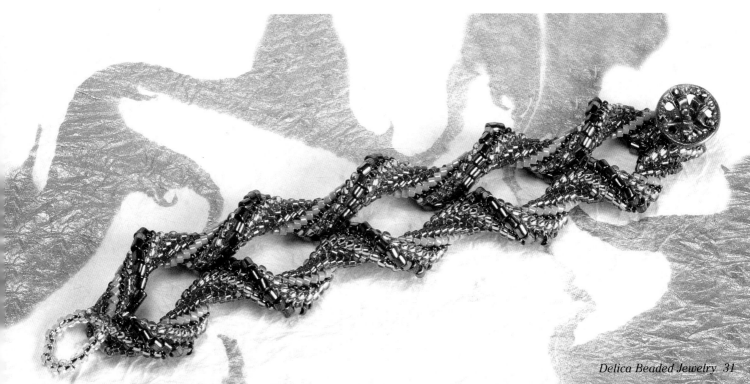

Jewel of the Pyramids

Surface Embellishments on Brick Stitch Triangles

Starting simply as a strand of graduated brick stitch triangles, this necklace can be embellished as much or as little as you wish.

The fully embellished version uses size 15/0 seed beads to outline the color changes on the size 10 Delica triangles, which causes them to form a puffed shape. It's finished with bottom, then top, edging using size 15/0 and 11/0 seed beads and 3 and 4mm crystals so it curves gracefully. A fancy sterling silver fairy clasp from Green Girl Studios completes the design.

By omitting the surface embellishment of the triangles, this necklace is easy enough for a beginner.

Materials

10-12g Delica, size 10, silver-lined purple, #1204 (dark/D)
5g Delica, size 10, silver-lined lavender, #146 (medium/M)
5g Delica, size 10, satin silver-lined dusty rose, #191 (light/L)
7g Miyuki seed beads, size 11/0, blue with purple luster, #460 (dark/D)
7g Miyuki seed beads, size 11/0, silver-lined lavender, #12 (medium/M)
7-10g Miyuki seed beads, size 15/0, blue with purple luster, #460 (dark/D)
5-7g Miyuki seed beads, size 15/0, silver-lined lavender, #12 (medium/M)
5g Miyuki seed beads, size 15/0, copper-lined opal, #198 (light/L)
41 Swarovski bicone crystals, 4mm, amethyst champagne
20 Swarovski bicone crystals, 3mm, amethyst
21 Swarovski bicone crystals, 3mm, light amethyst
Sterling silver Fairy hook clasp by GreenGirlStudios.com
2 Sterling silver split rings, 4-6mm
2 Sterling silver clamshell bead tips
G-S Hypo Cement
Beading cord such as Stringth or Silkon, size 1 or 2
Beading thread, K-O purple or Nymo B
Beading needles sizes 12 and 13
Twisted wire beading needles
2 Bead Stoppers, small size or small thread clamps

How-to

The order for making this necklace sounds complicated, but it is the most straightforward method. I tend to bead with long thread, 2-3 yds. (1.8-2.7m), but use shorter thread if you have tangling problems, and end a thread if it begins to fray. Although K-O beading thread is very fray-resistant, the surface embellishment part of this project is hard on any thread, especially if it is too long.

Avoid knots as much as possible; instead weave the thread through 3 beads twice in a crossing diagonal pattern to end or add it. Knots might make working the surface embellishment pattern impossible. But do not fill the beads with thread unnecessarily; you will have to go through them many more times for the surface and edge embellishments.

Starting the Triangle Base

Refer to Basic Tecniques on page 5 for brick stitch.

1. Using a twisted wire beading needle and doubled beading cord, string 14-15" (35.5-38cm) of dark size 10 Delicas, leaving the wire needle and at least 10" (25cm) of doubled cord on each end. Keep the beads together with Bead Stoppers against the end beads, and move the Stoppers as you work.

2. Fold the beaded cord in half to find the approximate center and begin the largest triangle so its center falls at that point. Work the triangles with size 10 Delicas.

3. Work the largest triangle (13-bead base row) at the center.

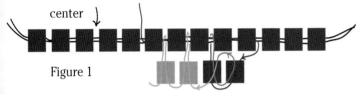

Figure 1

4. To begin the 13-bead base row of the first triangle. Thread a size 12 or 13 beading needle with as long a single length of K-O beading thread as you can use comfortably. Leaving a 6" (15cm) tail, pass the needle through about 5 beads from the center toward the first stitch of the first triangle. You'll weave this tail into the triangle to secure it so you don't later find yourself balked by impassable knots. Be careful not to pull it out as you work the first few stitches.

5. To work the base row, see "Brick stitch," figure 3, in Basic Techniques, page 5. Treat the strand of beads as if it were a ladder and sew around the cord between the beads on the strand as shown in figure 1.

a. With your needle exiting the strand at the center triangle's edge bead, pick up 2D, skip the next bead on the strand, working toward the center, and go around the cord between the second and third beads. Go back through the 2D, second bead first (photo 1 and chart at bottom left), and tighten the thread. Sew through the second bead toward the first and jiggle the thread as you tighten it so the beads stand up.

b. Pick up 1M for the third bead of the base row, sew under the cord after the next bead, and sew back through the new bead toward the previous stitch.

c. Begin each row of the triangle with 2 beads as in step a; then add the rest of the row's beads one at a time.

d. When you have added the single bead at the tip of the triangle, embellish the surface as described below.

e. Finish the triangle by going up through the outer edge bead on its base row toward the strand. Go through 2 beads on the strand and begin the next triangle.

6. Continue making triangles in the following order to the end of the cord. If needed, string more beads.

See the triangle charts here and on page 34: 11-bead triangle, 9-bead triangle, 11-bead triangle, 9-bead triangle, 7-bead triangle, 9-bead triangle, 7-bead triangle, 5-bead triangle, 7-bead triangle, 5-bead triangle.

End with 3 dark size 10 Delicas and the Bead Stopper.

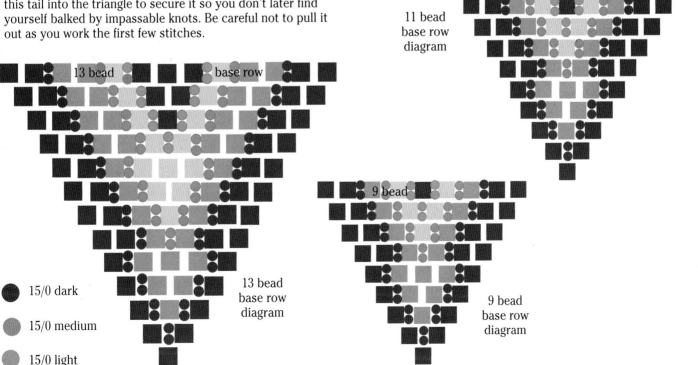

11 bead base row

11 bead base row diagram

9 bead

9 bead base row diagram

13 bead base row

13 bead base row diagram

● 15/0 dark

● 15/0 medium

● 15/0 light

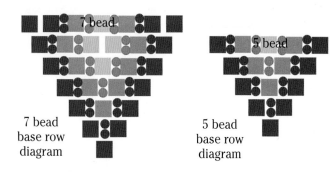

7 bead

5 bead

7 bead
base row
diagram

5 bead
base row
diagram

7. For a shorter necklace, omit the last or last two triangles on each end. To lengthen the necklace, simply string more dark size 10 Delicas on the ends of the cord. After finishing the last triangle on the first half of the necklace, work the bottom edging back to the center.

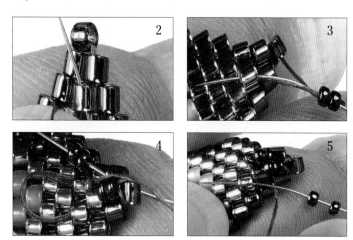

Triangle Surface Embellishment

I can't give you a perfect formula for surface embellishing each of the triangles. Expediency will take you in a variety of directions as you place 2 size 15/0 seed beads in the ditches between each color change on the triangles. Try not to backtrack too much so you don't overfill any of the size 10 Delicas.

Place pairs of 15/0D in each of the ditches between the medium and dark Delicas. Use 15/0M pairs in the ditches between medium and light Delicas and 15/0L pairs in the ditches that outline the dark Delicas at the top center of the larger triangles.

1. After adding the tip bead, your needle is going through a bead on the 2-bead row. Continue up the edge bead on the next row, then go down the middle bead of this row (photo 2).

Pick up 2 size 15/0D and sew through the tip bead toward the other bead on the 2-bead row. This stitch needs to be centered so sew back up the 2 embellishment beads and into the middle bead on the 3-bead row to fill the ditch on the 2-bead row (photo 3).

2. Sew up the bead to its left or right on the 4-bead row then down the other M bead on this row. Pick up 2D 15/0s and sew down the bead directly below the one you are exiting on the 4-bead row – the edge bead on the 2-bead row – to fill the ditch between colors on the 3-bead row (photo 4).

3. Go up the other bead on the 2-bead row, pick up 2D 15/0s, and sew up the bead above it on the 4-bead row (photo 5).

4. I tend to work up the far side from the next triangle to be woven, fill in the center spaces, then work back up the side where the new triangle will begin. Even so, I have to do some backtracking to fill all the ditches.

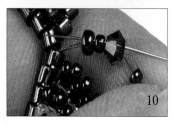

Bottom Edging

You use mostly size 15/0 dark seed beads for the bottom edging. The only exception is 2 size 11/0 dark seed beads on the tip crystal and one on the top crystal.

See the charts on p. 33 and above for embellishment patterns.

1. If a long thread remains after you've embellished the last triangle at the first end, you can use it to begin the bottom edging. Otherwise, end it and start a new thread in the end triangle, exiting the outer edge bead on the base row toward the triangle's tip.

2. Pick up 3 size 15/0D and sew back through the same edge bead and the next edge bead in a backstitch (photo 6).

3. Pick up 2 size 15/0D for the next backstitch. Go through the last seed bead of the previous stitch then the second and third edge beads on the triangle (photo 7).

4. Repeat step 3 twice more to complete the first side of the triangle, and go through the point bead.

5. For the drop on the point, pick up an 11/0D, a 15/0D, a 4mm crystal, and a 15/0D.

Skip the last seed bead and sew back through the crystal and the 15/0 above it (photo 8).

6. Pick up an 11/0D and sew through the triangle's point bead again toward the unedged side. Continue through the first edge bead (photo 9).

7. Start edging this side as in step 2 and make the remaining 3 edging stitches as in step 3.

8. When you've edged the top bead of the first triangle, sew through the strand bead after it. For the top drop, pick up an 11/0D, a 15/0D, a 3mm amethyst crystal, and a 15/0D. Sew back up the crystal and the 2 beads above it (photo 10).

9. Tighten the drop and go through the next strand bead and the first edge bead of the next triangle (photo 11).

10. Continue edging until you've added the top drop after the 13-bead triangle.